S THE WAY OF THE HEPHERD

Scripture quotations are from the New American Standard Bible, © The Lockman Foundation 1960, 1962, 1963, 1968, 1971, 1972, 1973, 1975, 1977. Used by permission.

Photography by Åke Lundberg

THE WAY OF THE SHEPHERD
© 1987 by Don Baker
Published by Multnomah Press
Portland, Oregon 97266

Multnomah Press is a ministry of Multnomah School of the Bible, 8435 NE Glisan Street, Portland, OR 97220

Printed in Singapore

Library of Congress Cataloging-in-Publication Data

Baker, Don.
    The way of the shepherd

    Bibliography: p.
    1. Bible. O. T. Psalms XXIII—Meditations.   I. Title.
BS1450 23rd.B25 1987   242'.5   87-5699
ISBN 0-88070-193-5 (pbk.)

87 88 89 90 91 92 93 94 – 8 7 6 5 4 3 2 1

Don Baker

S THE WAY OF THE HEPHERD

*Courage and Contentment
from the 23rd Psalm*

MULTNOMAH · PRESS
Portland, Oregon 97266

To John and Kathryn
Two Lambs
Entrusted to our care for awhile
and now shepherding their own.

"The Lord Is My Shepherd . . ."

*S*hepherds are people who watch over sheep.

SHEPHERDS REALLY HAVEN'T CHANGED MUCH in the thirty centuries since David wrote his Pastoral Psalm.

The shepherd's rod and staff remain the same—a rifle has been added.

Flowing, loose-fitting robes have been exchanged for bib overalls or Levi's in some parts of the world.

Nikes and boots cover the feet in place of the old, flimsy, loose-fitting sandals.

In some countries, motorized vehicles have taken the place of the obstinate burro, or the calloused feet.

Other than that, shepherding really hasn't changed much.

There have always been good shepherds, not-so-good shepherds, bad shepherds and very bad shepherds, and sheep always seem to know the difference.

Sheep will stay close to a good shepherd—one who displays confidence and quietness; but they will stay hundreds of unfriendly yards away from that shepherd who appears anxious or insecure. They will keep their distance from the unknowing and the uncaring.

A good shepherd has always been required to stay alert twenty-four hours each day. Sleeping with one eye and both ears open, he listens for the bleats, the bells, and the dogs that would warn of any danger or restlessness among his flock.

A shepherd is responsible for the total welfare of his sheep. Sheep are dependent for their food, their water, their health, and their safety. A shepherd can have no other vocation. Shepherding is an around-the-clock job with no respite, no reprieve.

If shepherds haven't changed much over the centuries, SHEEP HAVE CHANGED EVEN LESS.

Sheep are still among the world's most wonderful animals, providing
> wool for clothing,
>> mutton, the most digestible of all meats,
>>> milk for childhood diseases,
>>>> lanolin for hundreds of uses, and
>>>>> soft sheepskin blankets for the sick
>>>>> and the elderly.

As wondeful as they are, they still are stupid, unreasoning, irascible, unpredictable animals. Their flock mentality makes herding easy at times, and at other times, nearly impossible. When one restless sheep moves, the whole flock can move. When one old ewe sinks to the ground to chew her cud, the others follow.

Sheep are still defenseless—unable to protect themselves. They are often the victims of the wild animals that surround them.

They still don't know the difference between poisonous and non-poisonous plants.

Today's sheep have learned little since David the shepherd-boy tended them long centuries ago.

As much as we dislike doing it, we all must admit to some unflattering similarities with these dumb animals. Every time we see those thick-bodied, four-legged creatures lined up nose to tail in that strange woolie procession with their heads nodding in unison, we see ourselves.

We are not sheep and sheep are not people, but we are *like* sheep. There is a strange affinity.

SHEPHERDS HAVEN'T CHANGED MUCH—

SHEEP HAVE CHANGED EVEN LESS—

THE LORD HASN'T CHANGED AT ALL.

Three thousand years has made no difference whatever with God.

That's one reason Psalm 23 is still the best-known and most-loved chapter in the Bible.

That's why the page on which it rests is so worn.

That's why we instinctively turn to it when needs arise.

That's why we
  memorized it as children,
    recited it as youths,
      taught it to our own,
        repeat it in our advancing age, and
          cling to it in our death.

Every generation can identify with sheep.

Every culture can visualize a tender shepherd.

Every age can trust the Changeless One and find warmth and shelter in the constant love and care He provides for His flock.

"The Lord Is My Shepherd . . ."

*T*wenty to fifty sheep are called a bunch.

One hundred to one thousand, a flock.

One thousand and more are referred to as a band. A band of sheep can stretch out for miles, be herded by many dogs, and be led by a nanny goat or bellwether ram. But they will tolerate only one lead shepherd.

Most shepherds work alone.

Shepherds have long been aware of the dangers of being alone with their sheep. Some have been known to become "sheeped," or go insane from loneliness, sandstorms, or the never-ending heat.

Shepherds have been bitten by rattlesnakes and, unable to tend their own wounds, have died. Some have accidentally set their own clothes afire and have burned to death. Others have fallen into steep ravines and have been unable to escape.

David addressed his loneliness with his harp. He spent hours perfecting his slinging arm. He learned to hurl his rod with precision accuracy. He sang to his sheep. Others have whittled with sharp knives on their staffs. Some have built little rock monuments or have carved their names along with sentimental sayings on the trunks of trees.

They are alone and they work alone.

They alone know the names and habits of each of their sheep.

To me, all sheep look alike. But not to the experienced shepherd. He can locate one sheep out of twenty-five hundred in less than five minutes time. He can tell the difference by the way they hold their heads or by the way they walk.

The experienced shepherd can distinguish the lost, the ill, or the mother in search of her lost lamb.

Each one bleats differently.

The shepherd learns to read the signs of the bedding-down place. He knows where each sheep has slept. As he looks at the ground he can tell if the sheep is sick by the condition of its dung, or by dropped horns, or drops of blood that have been left behind.

Each flock of sheep has its own lead shepherd.

WE HAVE BUT ONE SHEPHERD.

There are many undershepherds, and I am one of them, but we have but one lead Shepherd.

The Psalm begins with the three-letter word *the*—a word that in this Psalm is used to designate uniqueness. The word identifies the shepherd of the Twenty-third as the one and only,

>the unique,
>>the incomparable,
>>>the different.

WE HAVE BUT ONE SHEPHERD.

There is no hierarchy, no chain of command among the shepherds of the spiritual flock.

Our Shepherd never delegates His responsibility to another.

He never dispatches subordinates to care for us.

He alone, despite the immensity of the task, knows us, understands us, and watches over us. He is constantly aware of each individual need.

Our Shepherd is always available.

He never gets "sheeped." He is never disabled. He never even gets lonely.

Israel, in David's day, was unique among all the nations of the world. It had but one God.

Egypt was a land of many gods. It had 360 primary gods—one for each day of the Egyptian calendar year. The surrounding hostile nations of the Land of Canaan had many gods. David slew one of them with a rock from his ever-present sling (1 Samuel 17:48-50).

David had but one God.

There was and is no other like Him.

There need be no other like Him.

He stands alone and above all others.

He shepherds a band of sheep—two thousand plus a few hundred million more.

He displays
   constant alertness,
      continuing awareness, and
         incomparable power.

We have but one Shepherd.

One is all we need.

"The Lord Is My Shepherd . . ."

$\mathcal{S}$hepherding has never been the most honored profession in the world.

Ancient Egyptians regarded it as the lowest. An Egyptian would have nothing to do with sheep. For Moses to step down from the throne as Egypt's Pharaoh-Elect to the position of one of Jethro's shepherds was the ultimate insult.

The youngest son, in Bible times, was given the demeaning task of tending the sheep. David and Joseph were the last-born and were given the job. In families where sons were not available, the task went to daughters.

And yet—some well-known names comprise the list of earth's shepherds.

Abraham,
  Isaac,
    Jacob,
      Moses,
        David,
          God.

God Is a Shepherd.

The host of heaven must marvel at the Creator-God who daily walks among the lowliest of His creation—the Majestic Sovereign who leaves the command center of the universe to roam the hillsides of earth at the head of His band of dependent sheep.

God Is a Shepherd.

"Lord" is His name—His personal name.

That's the name He gave to Moses when asked to identify Himself. It appears for the first time in human history in the third chapter of Exodus, and then reappears four thousand times on the pages that follow.

It is the Name that is transliterated "Jehovah."

It appears throughout our Bibles as LORD, spelled out in capital letters.

It means "I AM WHO I AM."

IT TEACHES THAT OUR SHEPHERD IS TIMELESS.

He is not confined by the boundaries of time nor limited by the resources He Himself has created.

Our Shepherd fills all of time with the magnitude of His presence. He then spills out over the boundaries of time to fill all of eternity.

He lives in the eternal "now." That means that He has not only walked through all of our yesterdays, lived in all of our todays, but He has already experienced all of our tomorrows.

Since He already knows tomorrow's agenda, He has already made provision for it.

HE IS NOT ONLY TIMELESS, BUT HE IS ALSO TOTALLY FREE.

He is dependent upon no one.

He is the only totally independent being in the universe. He is self-contained, self-perpetuating.

He is not dependent upon the daylight to see nor upon the sun to be warmed. He requires no food for sustenance and no rest for replenishment. He needs no outside source for wisdom or external force for strength.

He exists by Himself. He is self-existent.

And,
    if he needs help from no one,
    if He knows no limitations,
    if all that will ever be needed is already
        present in His own Being,
then,
    He can be to us, His sheep, all that we will
        ever need.

Notice, I did not say that "He will provide for all of our needs." He will do that, too. I said, "*He will be to us* all that we will ever need." If I have nothing but my Lord, I have everything I need.

The condition of every flock is determined by the shepherd who tends it. Sheep are unable to meet their own needs. But then, they don't need to.

The LORD is my shepherd.

"The Lord Is My Shepherd . . ."

Count the words in the Twenty-third Psalm.

The number will vary according to the version. In my Bible there are 115. Of the 115, 92 are but one syllable.

Shepherds only talk to sheep in words of one syllable.

If a herder wishes to get a quick response from the sheep, he will impersonate the sheep's cry for salt. The words are more like a flutter, and sound like *ru-ru-ru-ru-ru-ru-ru*. With this cry a shepherd can lead his flock quickly from the presence of danger.[1]

The water call is a repetition of one syllable words, *meee-maaa-meee-maaa*. When the shepherd mocks this cry, he had better stand clear. The water call can cause thirsty sheep to stampede.[2]

Shepherds only talk to sheep in words of one syllable.

Shepherds cannot afford to give confusing signals. The safety of the flock may depend on it. The security of the flock may be at stake.

Nearly nine out of every ten words in Psalm 23 are words of one syllable.

It seems that our Shepherd wants to be understood.

The safety and the security of His flock are at stake.

Simplicity is not a mark of ignorance. It is a sign of profound intelligence. This Psalm is deceptively simple. It could lead one to think that it is simplistic.

Simple it is, simplistic it is not.

Simple minds need simple expressions to comprehend complex truth. The truths contained in these 115 words are so profound and limitless that to understand and believe them is to understand and believe in God.

To embrace these truths is to live forever.

The word MY is but one syllable—just two letters. It is the most wonderfully intimate of all the words in the Psalm.

It is personal.

It is possessive.

It's the sweetest word in the Psalm.

The Lord is A shepherd—true.

The Lord is THE shepherd—true.

The Lord is the GOOD shepherd—true.

The Lord is the CHIEF shepherd—true.

But, He is more. The Lord is MY Shepherd.

It constantly amazes me that our Lord can head a band of sheep that's beyond number—that stretches across nations and encompasses earth, and yet never once lose sight of me.

A shepherd is active in every moment of a sheep's life: from its birth—often serving as midwife, to its death—when he devises the swiftest, most painless death possible.

He provides for its food. He gently pulls thorns from its fleece and thistles from its paws. He painlessly shears wool from its body—and even gently sets leg bones when they're broken.

Sheep often nuzzle the shepherd in their own limited expression of gratitude.

My Shepherd knows me in every phase of my life.

He knows my name.

He knows my need.

He knows my wants.

He knew me before I was born.

He shaped me in my mother's womb.

He assisted in my delivery.

He knows my thoughts before I think them,
　　　　my words before I speak them, and
　　　　my actions before I perform them.

He has counted each hair on my head.

He has measured my height.

He monitors my heartbeat and blood pressure.

He remembers the date of my birth.

He even knows the date of my death, and has already made provision for that event.

The Lord is MY Shepherd.

That one little word *my* moves the shepherd-sheep relationship into something deeply personal.

The Lord is MY shepherd. Oh, He's yours too.

But that in no way interferes with or diminishes His relationship with me. Our Shepherd is big enough to embrace us each and embrace us all. In embracing us all, there is no less love or concern for one than the other.

It's quite common for the lesser to claim the greater. Man has always boasted of his gods. We boast in our God. When we say, "the Lord is MY Shepherd," we're engaging in name-dropping in its ultimate form.

What's really startling is when the greater claims the lesser—when God boasts in man—when Jesus claims us as His own.

He reverses the relationship in John 10:14 and calls us HIS sheep.

To claim the Lord as MY shephed is the supreme act of faith.

To be claimed by the Lord as His sheep is the ultimate act of grace.

He is MY shepherd.

1. Louis Irigaray and Theodore Taylor, *A Shepherd Watches, A Shepherd Sings* (New York: Doubleday & Company, 1977), p. 29
2. Ibid., p. 27

". . . I Shall Not Want"

*S*heep really don't need much.

They need food.

Shepherds are in constant search of lush meadows where the flock can graze. Sheep love to graze in fields of pepper and alfilaria grass. They like thick heavy carpets of green, sweet grass checked with orange poppy and lupin and wild marigolds. A shepherd will often taste the grass to test its sweetness before feeding it to his flock.

They need water.

A sheep's vitality and strength is determined by its intake of water. When sheep are deprived of adequate water, dehydration sets in and the animal becomes weak. A shepherd will mark the water holes, remember the springs and streams, and make sure that his animals have ample supply.

They need rest.

Rest is essential to the production of fleece and mutton. It's essential in bearing healthy lambs. Rest is impossible when food or water are in short supply. Rest is impossible in the presence of fear or anxiety.

They need protection.

The shepherd is their sole source of protection. He must remain constantly alert to impure water, improper food, and prowling animals intent upon the destruction of the sheep.

Sheep really don't need much. Just food, water, rest, and protection—like people.

They often want more than they need. Their cravings can make them drunk if they eat too many grapes, sick if they drink polluted water, or kill them if they bloat themselves with too much alfalfa. If they wander from the flock in an attempt to satisfy an insatiable craving, a prowler can destroy them.

A shepherd is forced to constantly watch and listen for signs of restlessness. Bells are hung around the the necks of the discontented. The tranquil, quiet, contented sheep needs no bell.

Often at night, awakening from sleep, the shepherd learns to read what sounds like the Morse code of the bells. A single clang of the clapper means that a discontented sheep is trudging off. It may be in search of greener pastures or purer water. If the clang is rapid, it means she's running—sometimes from danger, but usually, she is just dissatisfied.[1]

Some sheep are so restless, so discontented, so perverse, that destruction is the only solution to their bad habits. In spite of the shepherd's provision, it becomes necessary to kill the wanderer in order to spare the flock.

Contented sheep are a proud tribute to a competent shepherd.

CONTENTED BELIEVERS ARE A PROUD TRIBUTE TO A SATISFYING CHRIST.

A lasting memory for me is that of my grandmother serenely sitting in the family rocking chair, peering through variety store eyeglasses at the large print of a big Bible on her lap.

She was old, diabetic, widowed, and poor. Her little house consisted of a kitchen, living room, bedroom, and bath.

Her church was across the street.

She walked two blocks to cash her meager welfare check and pay her utilities. Her groceries were delivered to the back door.

Her kitchen stove burned wood. Her oil heater needed constant regulating. The uncarpeted floor was always drafty. The roof leaked. The lawn was in need of care.

She had buried parents, husband, two of her twelve children, and even some of her grandchildren. All of her living children had long since left town—many of them hundreds of miles away.

But I never heard her complain. She was content.

Whenever I'd ask if I could get her anything, the answer was always the same:

"I have everything I need."

In this greedy grasping world of ours, that sort of contentment is rare.

That kind of contentment is irresistibly attractive to the people of the world who think that wealth consists of the abundance of things, rather than the absence of wants.

Sheep are branded by their owners. This may consist of burning by an iron, marking the skin with dye, or cutting a notch in an ear. The animal is always recognized by the brand.

God's people are known by their brand.

Contentment, the ability to live with little and be satisfied, marks us as His.

"I shall not want" simply means, "I have everything I need."

1. Irigaray, p. 13

"He Makes Me Lie Down . . ."

*S*heep will graze until sundown, their necks bowed toward earth, their jaws constantly busy—nibbling and chewing, nibbling and chewing.

Some will stand erect for a while in the darkness and then, finally, reluctantly fold their knees and settle to earth with an audible sigh.

Once a flock is bedded down, they usually stay unless disturbed by a human or a four-legged prowler.

A full moon will sometimes cause them to be restless.

Hunger can cause a gluttonous ewe to rise and roam in search of a snack.

Sheep are totally ignorant of their own limitations. When frightened they will run until stopped or until they drop.

When chased by a predator, they will run until they fall from exhaustion. Sometimes that exhaustion results in death.

A careful shepherd will gauge the limitations of his flock. He will gauge the traveling distance and make certain his sheep are not allowed to overextend themselves.

It is often necessary to force the sheep to rest.

A dear friend, who had lived most of his adult life in the fast lane was forced to "lie down."

He was anxious, bewildered, frustrated. He was convinced, like most of us, that he was indispensable and immortal. He asked me numerous times from his hospital bed, "Pastor, why is God doing this to me? I don't have time for this. It makes no sense whatever. It just couldn't have come at a worse time."

As I listened, frustration oozed out of every pore in his body. He tossed aimlessly. I saw the helpless look in his eyes.

I began to quote the Twenty-third Psalm to him.

As soon as I began to speak those well-known words I noticed a look of bored resignation come over him. A feeling of disgust was evident. He knew the Psalm. He knew it well. He was convinced that nothing new could be offered from something so familiar.

"I think I need a new truth for this one, pastor. I'm afraid that Psalm has little to say to me tonight."

I quoted,

> The Lord is my shepherd, I shall not want.
> He makes me lie down in green pastures . . . .

I quoted it again—nothing more, just those two lines.

> The Lord is my shepherd, I shall not want.
> He makes me LIE DOWN in green pastures . . . .

I quoted it again, and again.

Each time he looked at me and wondered what in the world I was trying to say.

I emphasized each word in the second line over and over again until I finally said to him,

> HE MAKES ME lie down . . . .

My friend looked up in amazement. "I've never noticed that before," he said. "Is that why I'm here? Are you saying that God has *put me here*—that He is the one responsible for this?"

"Certainly," I answered. "You believe that God is sovereign, don't you? You believe that He is the gracious controller of all things, don't you?"

"Yes," he answered.

"If that's true, then aren't we forced to conclude that God is in charge of this frustrating moment? Aren't you here, forced to lie down, because God has decided that this is what He wants you to do at this point in time?"

Tears formed. They spilled over the outside of each eye, trickled down through his sideburns and settled in each ear.

He relaxed.

"Thank you Father," he said.

A fast-paced chief executive officer of a thriving corporation had finally realized that his gentle but insistent Shepherd had pulled him over for a much needed rest—a time on his back when the only direction he could look was up.

It's possible for people to act like sheep—to ignore the signs of weariness—to the point of exhaustion. It is during these times that the Shepherd must make the decision that it's time to rest.

Without His intervention we might continue to grind the starter until the battery is dead—to run the engine until the tank is dry. The overheating that comes as a result of unending stress can be fatal.

Life is like a symphony. It has its moments of music and its moments of silence. Sounds, followed by pauses. Moments of energy interrupted by moments of rest.

OUR SHEPHERD KNOWS WHEN IT'S TIME TO REST.

He's in charge of the pauses, the interludes, the restful moments of silence.

He knows when. He knows how.

There are times when it is necessary to stop in order to be able to start again.

". . . HE MAKES ME LIE DOWN . . . ."

"He Makes Me Lie Down In Green Pastures . . ."

*G*reen pastures don't "just happen."

If ever you've walked over the rolling hills of Israel, you've noted that the ground is rocky, barren and brown.

Lack of rain between May and October means that vegetation is either withered in the heat or non-existent. In the shepherds' fields near Bethlehem where David grazed his flock, the earth is dry and scorched by the sun.

Green pastures are non-existent unless someone— usually the shepherd—has already gone to the trouble of clearing the rocks, plowing the soil, planting the seed, irrigating the land, and carefully tending the grasses to be certain that his sheep have what they need.

When it comes time to lie down, sheep need green pastures.

GREEN PASTURES DON'T JUST HAPPEN— THEY'RE CAUSED.

Green pastures are the shepherd's provision for the flock when the lambs are small and the milk demand on the ewes is great.

To a shepherd, there are few things in life more rewarding than to watch his sheep sprawled beneath the summer sun with bellies full from a morning of munching on the rich green grass.

By skillfully managing the soil, it is possible for lambs to gain as much as one hundred pounds in weight during their first one hundred days of life. All they need is rest from trailing, and lush pasture that allows them to fill up quickly and then lie down to rest and chew their cud.

For me, the trailing times have not been the growing times.

Most often I have grown the most when taken away from the grinding demands of a heavy work load. I'm often hustled out of my spirituality—sometimes to the point of exhaustion. It's then that I'm forced to rest. The forced rests that occur when HE MAKES ME LIE DOWN are often humiliating and painful.

When the steel doors to the psychiatric ward* of the veteran's hospital slammed shut behind me years ago, I saw myself in a barren, desolate place. It first appeared to be a place of death rather than a place of life.

As I walked through the door to Ward 7E, my one thought was that the life I had known was finished. I would never again be able to enjoy the confidence of a congregation who would trust me to shepherd them.

For days I withdrew into a medicated stupor. I resented sharing a room with one patient who was criminally insane and another who walked around like a zombie.

I refused all offers of help. I resisted any intrusions into my silence. I rejected the many opportunities to visit with friends.

I was unable to pray and unwilling to try.

The wells of Scripture dried up. Try as I might, it was impossible to satisfy a dried-up spirit.

God had withdrawn or taken a vacation—I didn't know which—and I was left alone, I thought, to die.

What a God-forsaken place to be forced to "lie down," I thought.

It was not forsaken, however. God *was* there. He had already made provision for me.

The barren, rocky soil had already been broken up. The seed had been planted and the grasses had already begun to sprout, and for weeks I feasted on the presence of God and the provisions that had been awaiting my arrival.

*For a full account, see *Depression: Finding Hope & Meaning in Life's Darkest Shadow* (Multnomah Press, 1983).

In that pasture I gained new friends. I discovered
    a new compassion for the hurting,
    a new strategy in counseling,
    a new insight into communication.

I had gotten to know and to trust myself.

I had gotten to know and to trust God.

I was more calm, more confident, and the physical problem that had limited me for so long was finally under control.

A barren place? That's the way it looked going in.

A green pasture? That's what it turned out to be, and as I look back on it I see it as one of the most significant growing times of my entire life.

"HE MAKES ME LIE DOWN IN GREEN PASTURES...."

"He Leads Me Beside Quiet Waters . . ."

Sheep usually stay quiet. The limited sounds they do make are not discernible to a stranger. To a shepherd, however, sheep-talk is readily understood.

A ewe in search of her lamb makes a distinctive sound.

Bleating ewes at dusk make a much different sound.

When sheep need salt in their diet, they have a special bleat.

The bleat for water is different still.

Thirsty sheep can quickly become unmanageable. If water is unavailable, they may run for miles to where they remember being watered a year before.[1]

A sheep's body is composed of about 70 percent water. The fluid which is stored in the animal's cells is used to maintain a normal body metabolism and is essential to its good health.

Sheep drink from springs, rivers, water holes. They can survive for long periods of time without these sources, however, if the shepherd rises up early enough to encourage the sheep to eat the dew-laden grasses.[2]

The morning dew is the purest water available.

Before they can drink from a quiet water hole, it is often necessary for the shepherd to clear away the debris and pollution.

In many places, water doesn't just happen, either. At times it is pulled from cisterns or deep wells and poured out into drinking troughs.

Thirsty sheep can only be satisfied at the expense of the tireless efforts of the shepherd.

In every flock there are stubborn ewes and lambs that stop to drink the filthy, polluted waters from muddy pools along the trails. The water can be contaminated with the urine and manure of sheep that have already passed that way. The stubborn still believe it to be the only, or at least the best available.

Twenty five hundred years ago, the LORD described a condition that still prevails today. He said, "My people have committed two evils; they have forsaken Me, the fountain of living waters, to hew for themselves cisterns, broken cisterns that can hold no water" (Jeremiah 2:13).

For us insatiably thirsty sheep, with cravings almost too great to satisfy, our Shepherd not only leads us to the water, but He *is* the water.

Jesus leads us to Himself, the source of the pure, thirst-quenching, soul-satisfying water of life. And then He invites us to drink freely, without cost (Revelation 22:17).

Jesus, our Shepherd, said, ". . . whoever drinks of the water that I shall give him shall never thirst; but the water that I shall give him shall become in him a well of water springing up to eternal life" (John 4:14).

Only Jesus can satisfy our soul's thirst.

1. Irigaray, p. 28.
2. Phillip Keller, *A Shepherd Looks at Psalm 23* (Grand Rapids: Mich.: Zondervan, 1970), p. 50.

"He Restores My Soul"

*I*n its utter helplessness, a "cast" sheep will die unless the shepherd moves in quickly to save it.

During our early years of ministry, we lived in the country adjacent to a sheep ranch. We watched the sheep daily with great interest.

From a distance they all looked alike. Our untrained eyes were unable to detect the many distinctive markings that made each of the animals unique from the others.

We would watch them and count them and laugh at them and marvel at them as we became familiar with their antics.

Early one morning, I saw a ewe on its back with all four legs sticking straight up in the air. I walked out into the field, examined it carefully, nudged it with my toe and then went back in the house to call the owner.

"One of your sheep is dead," I told him.

He arrived within a few minutes, walked over to the sheep, knelt down beside it and then called me to join him.

"This sheep isn't dead," he said. "This sheep is only cast. Watch me, Don, and I'll show you something about sheep."

He took hold of the outstretched, stiffening limbs and began vigorously massaging them. As he worked with the unmoving body he explained, "Often when a sheep is heavy with lamb or heavy with wool, it will lie down on uneven ground and then roll over on its back into a shallow recess. When it does, it's like a beetle, unable to rise or roll over by itself. On its back, the gases will gather, the limbs will stiffen and it won't be long before it will die."

I watched as he massaged each of those four out-stretched legs, rubbing them firmly up and down. He would alternately rub his hands briskly over the full length of its body.

As he continued, the muscles began to twitch. The body began to move and I saw the unmistakable signs of life.

It wasn't long before that sheep was rolled over on its side and its weakened legs began to flail.

The gentle but insistent shepherd finally locked both hands under its belly, lifted it to its feet and began to walk it. The legs pawed aimlessly and wobbled weakly. It would have fallen were it not for the strong arms that held it.

After considerable time, the sheep was released. It ambled slowly in the direction of the grazing flock, joined them, and proceeded to feed with the rest. Later, as I searched for it, I was unable to distinguish it from the rest.

I had seen a "cast" sheep.

I had watched as a "cast" sheep was restored.

I had watched a ewe, in its abject helplessness, preserved from death by the intervention of its shepherd.

We are not sheep, but we are like sheep, and like sheep, there are times when we are unable to survive without the help of our Shepherd.

David uses the word "cast" in the King James Version in Psalm 42:5, 6. He addressed his helplessness as he poses a question to his depressed soul.

He asks,

"Why art thou cast down, O my soul?"

And again,

"O my God, my soul is cast down within me. . . ."

The apostle Paul uses the same word in 2 Corinthians 4:9. He describes his great unrest of soul at being unable to find Titus, his traveling companion.

The word *cast* is translated "despair." It refers to that time when the soul is bowed down, unable to lift itself, in a state of hopeless depression.

Words like,

sad
    empty
        alone
            hopeless
          afraid
              worthless
                  ambivalent
                rejected

completely dominate the horizon of our feelings.

Eating is difficult. Sleep is impossible. Unrestrained anger is followed by consuming guilt. Confusion prevails.

God is nowhere.

Life is over. Unless someone intervenes, we will attempt to turn that feeling into reality.

OUR LORD IS THE SOUL DOCTOR.

He is the only One trained and experienced in the healing of the soul—the only one qualified to determine just what remedy is needed and then to gently lift the "cast" soul back to life.

Man has discovered many remedies for ailing bodies, but only God can restore the soul.

The diseases of the soul are different from those of the body. The soul can be infected by guilt, restlessness, discouragement, depression, loneliness, emptiness, and the absence of hope. These diseases respond to the healing touch of the Savior as He applies His grace to our sin.

When we are missing from the flock, our Shepherd goes after the truant until He finds us and then lovingly, gently, but firmly restores us to the rest.

"HE RESTORES MY SOUL."

"HE RESTORES MY SOUL"

*S*heep, like people, not only need their shepherd, they need each other.

Sheep need to hear the tinkle or the clang of the nearby bells. They need to feel the presence of other bodies. They need to touch when they are "trailing" up and through the places of danger.

Sheep, like people, not only need their shepherd, they need each other.

I was awakened shortly after two o'clock one morning by the incessant ring of the telephone.

I mumbled a sleepy "hello."

"Pastor?" the voice asked. "This is Jeanie."

I was immediately awake. The voice was that of a distraught young mother—a new believer—whose life had suddenly become more than she could handle.

"It's time," she said.

"Is it?" I answered.

"Yes, I'm going to do it tonight."

"How Jeanie?"

"I've got it all figured out, and this time I won't fail."

"How do you plan to do it, Jeanie?"

"I've already done it. I just lit some briquets in the fireplace and closed the damper."

"Have you closed all the doors and windows?"

"Yes."

"Did you stuff them around the cracks so they'd be airtight?"

"Yes."

"Are you on the couch?"

"Yes."

"Are the children home?"

"No, they're at my sister's for the night."

"Is your husband working?"

"Yes, he won't be home until late in the morning."

"Have you written a note to the children?"

"No."

". . . to your husband?"

"No."

I could hear coughing as the room filled up with gaseous smoke.

"Are you sure you did the right thing in not leaving a note? They'll be very sad. They'll wonder why, you know. They'll probably blame themselves for your death."

There was no answer.

"Who'll be the first to come home in the morning?"

With great difficulty she coughed and said, "the children."

"Are you sure you want them to be the ones to find you?"

I listened to the choked sobs of a dying woman.

"Are you sure, Jeanie, that you've really thought of everything?"

There was silence and finally a scream. "Help me, I don't want the children to find me like this."

"Can you still move, Jeanie?"

"I think so."

"Can you roll off the couch onto the floor?"

"Yes."

"Don't let go of the phone. Hang on so you won't drop it. I want to talk to you some more."

I heard the distinctive "thud" as both she and the phone dropped to the floor.

"Are you still there?"

"Yes."

"Can you crawl to the front door and open it?"

"I'll try."

I heard the latch and the swing of the door in spite of the incessant coughing.

"Can you crawl over to the fireplace and open the damper?"

Step by step I led her from the door to the fireplace to the windows and back to the couch.

"Can you breathe better, Jeanie?"

"Yes."

"Is the smoke clearing?"

"Yes."

"Are you lying down?"

"Yes."

"Do you need a blanket?"

"No."

"Is the light still on?"

"Yes."

"Can you reach it? Don't hang up yet."

"Are you comfortable?"

"Yes."

"Do you think you can sleep now?"

"I think so."

"Before you hang up, let's pray."

I prayed with Jeanie, told her goodnight, hung up the phone and tried to go back to sleep.

The next morning she met me at the front door, fell into my arms and sobbed out the words, "Thank you, pastor. Thank you, thank you, thank you."

There are times when we not only need our shepherd, WE ALSO NEED EACH OTHER.

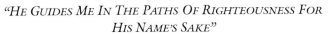

"He Guides Me In The Paths Of Righteousness For His Name's Sake"

An alert shepherd must be sensitive to his flock when trailing.

Moving the sheep from pasture to pasture or from lowland to highland requires great skill on the part of the shepherd.

Shepherds in the East usually walk ahead of their flocks.

Shepherds in the West usually walk behind.

Without the shepherd to pick out the acceptable grazing lands and then guide the flock into them, the sheep would soon destroy the fields and ultimately the sheep.

Sheep are creatures of habit. If they had their way, they would follow the same trails, graze the same hills, and pollute the same ground. The trails would soon become ruts, the hills would turn into wastelands, and the ground would be corrupted with disease.[1]

Sheep need to be managed. If left to themselves, they will gnaw the same grass until its gone. They will then paw at the ground to expose and unearth the roots. Eventually, only dust and rock will remain.

Guiding the sheep from one pasture to the next requires planning and close supervision.

"He guides me . . ." suggests that our Shepherd not only determines what direction is best for us, but He makes sure that we arrive at our appointed destination.

Several years ago my wife and I and two friends climbed Mt. Sinai. It required the services of one guide and one camel each for the four of us. The guides could have simply pointed us in the right direction and turned us loose, but they didn't.

There was more involved than just a destination.

Timing was important. We wanted to arrive at the right place at the right time. We wanted to see and to feel the sun as it rose over the magnificent peaks of Mt. Horeb.

Safety was a factor. To reach the peak at sunrise meant to climb the steep ravines in darkness. At times we could not see the ground beneath our animals. At other times we could, but wished we couldn't. The animals couldn't see the ground either; they felt it. I never knew that camels feel their way along rather than watch where they're going.

That was usually no problem, until they would walk with their hooves gliding along the edge of the precipitous cliff that fell hundreds of feet below us.

FEAR REQUIRED THE REASSURING PRESENCE OF OUR GUIDE.

None of us was experienced with camels. One of our riders was thrown. It was comforting to each of us to have a guide walking alongside.

We arrived safely and on time. We watched the same sun peak up over the same mountain and cast its same light over the same valleys that Moses had seen thirty-five hundred years before.

We would have missed it all without our guides.

Did you notice how the word *guide* provides a link between the two personal pronouns in verse three:

He GUIDES Me.

The distance between our Shepherd in heaven and us on earth may seem too great at times.

Our Lord may "feel" too far away to us.

The distance between God and me is bridged by the word *GUIDES*.

Our Guide knows where He wants to take us and He makes sure that we get there. Regardless of the distance, He never leaves our side.

Notice also, the destination is always the right one.

A shepherd never guides his sheep to destruction.

He never guides them into places that are polluted or overgrazed.

He never guides them into fields where food and water are not available.

He only guides them into the places that are right for them.

The "righteous path" is the path where both Shepherd and sheep are comfortable with each other.

Our Lord will never lead us in a direction that is incompatible with His nature. He will never lead us into sin.

He will only lead to those places where He can keep us.

Why? Because His reputation is at stake.

Sheep exist only for the sake of their owner. Their welfare is of primary concern since the loss of a sheep means loss, not to the sheep, but to the owner.

"For His name's sake" is amplified in John 10:27, 28 when Jesus says,

> My sheep hear My voice, and I know them,
> and they follow Me; and I give eternal life
> to them, and they shall never perish; and no
> one shall snatch them out of My hand.

The high price of the investment demands the absolute security of the flock.

God paid enough for each of us to cause Him to preserve us from anything that could destroy us.

FOR HIS SAKE, we are guided in the right direction and preserved until we reach HIS appointed destination.

---

1. Keller, p. 70.

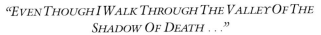

"EVEN THOUGH I WALK THROUGH THE VALLEY OF THE SHADOW OF DEATH . . ."

A "valley" is a place of fear—a place of danger.

For those of us who grew up around high mountains, valleys were always understood to be extensive lowlands or flatlands that usually stretch for miles between the peaks. The valleys were fertile and green and flat and safe.

David's valley is something altogether different. The valley referred to here is more like a ravine, and reminds us of the narrow, precipitous trails that stretch up through the wadis or draws from a mountain base to its top.

Valleys are always a challenge to a shepherd. They cause fear to the sheep.

Often led by a sure-footed nanny goat with a lead bell, the long single-file procession can stretch for miles.

Sheer drops of hundreds of feet can face the flock on one side and high walls with rocky crags hiding four-footed predators or snakes can rise up on the other.

Mountain trailing is a time of silence.

Only the clang of the bells and the plodding sound of the hooves can be heard. Any yelling, talking, or even singing can cause the sheep to panic. Even the dogs respect the need for silence.

Mountain lions have been known to unexpectedly spring across the trail causing the hysterical sheep to fall over the side and drop to their death.

Sheep are awesomely silent as they fall. There is no outcry when they strike the steep sides of the cliff or when they land at the bottom. Even with broken limbs, backs, or split bellies, they make no sound. When they fall, it becomes necessary for the herder to leave his flock, climb down the steep sides of the ravine, cut the throats of the dying and leave them for the buzzards.[1]

A "valley" is a place of fear—a place of danger.

Valleys are necessary.

The annual trek through the valley is the only way for the sheep to escape the barren, dry ground that has been parched by the summer sun or abused by over-grazing. The valley is the only way of escape from the relentless heat of the lowlands.

The valley is the only route to the high country.

Like sheep, most of us don't like the climb through the "valley."

"Valleys" represent a departure from the routine—an unexpected detour on the road of life.

The ultimate valley is death. Like all other valleys in life, however, it too, is designed to lift us higher.

Valleys are never appreciated while they are being endured.

No matter how many times the sheep climb the steep trails, they never lose their fear. The experience is both tedious and terrifying. Often it seems endless and impossible.

But the trip is always worth it.

A man asked his friend,

"How did you like your heart attack?"

"How did I like my heart attack?" the man replied. "What a foolish question!"

"But I understand you gained a new appreciation for life?"

"Yes, that's true."

". . . And I understand you're in better health now than you've ever been?"

"Yes."

". . . And I hear that your family ties are stronger than ever?"

"Yes."

". . . And you've gained a deeper love for your little granddaughter?"

"Yes."

". . . And you're learning to live with stress better than before?"

"Yes."

". . . And the Lord is more precious than you have ever known Him to be?"

"Yes, all those things are true."

"Let me ask you again, how did you like your heart attack?"

The only response was silence.

Valleys are often like heart attacks. The gain far exceeds the pain.

1. Irigaray, p. 3

"*V*alleys" are never happy prospects.

Some simple truths about valley experiences come into clear focus in this verse.

1. The Shepherd has planned the trip.

2. He has designed it to be temporary.

3. The fear is greater than the reality.

4. The Shepherd is always present.

5. The Shepherd is equipped to bring me safely through.

A trip through the "valley" is always by prearrangement.

It is never by coincidence—nor is it by accident.

It may appear to be either or both. It's neither.

In verse 2, the Shepherd LEADS me.

In verse 3, the Shepherd GUIDES me.

If the Shepherd is LEADING and GUIDING, then some of His travel plan must have included the "valley."

That's the dimension added to any and all of life's experiences when we begin to look at them through the lens of divine sovereignty.

My being in a "valley" can never be allowed to suggest that my Shepherd has abdicated His responsibility or lessened His control.

"Valleys" are planned. They are part of the trip through life.

"Valleys" are the only way to the highlands.

The highlands are where the sheep grow.

"Valleys" are planned.

An interesting rendition of Philippians 1:12 appears

in the King James Version of the Bible. It underscores this truth.

It reads,

> But I would ye should understand, brethren,
> that the things which happened unto me
> have fallen out rather unto the furtherance
> of the gospel.

Paul was in a "valley" when he wrote those words.

He was in Rome, in prison.

The words *which happened* were printed in the text in italics. That meant that they were not in the original manuscript.

Those two words provided an excellent springboard with which to dive into a presentation of God's sovereignty by saying, "Nothing JUST HAPPENS in the will of God."

One of the most frightening, yet instructive "valley" experiences ever recorded took place thirty-five hundred years ago. While living in the Land of Uz—the land presently known as Syria—Job was led into and through his "valley."

His is the account of one of earth's greatest men being stripped of everything—
>
> his children,
>   his wealth,
>   his reputation,
>   his health, and
>   his self-respect.

Even his wife deserted him.

Job was reduced to a whining, complaining outcast who was forced to live in a garbage dump with the dogs and the lepers.

The story is given contemporary meaning only when one realizes that his entire trip into the "valley" was by prearrangement.

God did not cause it. He did *allow* it, however.

God permits the "valleys" and then He uses them, despite their pain, to lift us higher.

Job's life, after the garbage dump, was elevated to heights he could never have known without the garbage dump.

As much as we wish otherwise, there is no such thing as instant maturity. We would all like to be air-lifted to spiritual gianthood. Quick success in the Christian life is foreign to Scripture.

Growing is slow and usually imperceptible.

Growing demands "valleys."

But, the "valleys" are pre-planned.

Our Shepherd plans the starting point, the route, and the destination.

He traces the entire trip in advance to make certain that nowhere does it exceed my limitations.

He determines the degree of danger and eliminates anything He considers deadly.

And then he guides me . . . to be certain I arrive safely.

*"V*alley" experiences are temporary.

The climb from the lowlands to the highlands may take hours. It may take days. It may take weeks. But however long it may take, it always ends.

The important word in this sentence is "Through."

Notice, it does not say

"Into the Valley" or
"Over to the Valley" or
"Down to the Valley" or
"Up to the Valley."

It says "Even though I walk Through the Valley."

The important word is "Through."

The "valley" is not a dead-end street.

It is not a cul-de-sac.

It, like a tunnel, has openings at both ends.

Whenever we enter a "valley," we can be certain that, in addition to an entrance, it also has an exit.

When I wrote of my experience with depression, I described it as my trip into a "black hole." Black holes are frightening.

From my "black hole," I could see nothing.

In my "black hole," I felt trapped. Escape seemed impossible.

Perhaps that is why the words of one doctor will always remain in my memory. After charting the symptoms and analyzing the test results, he said to me, "Mr. Baker, you are depressed. We don't know the reason, but I want you to know something. Depression is not terminal. It will run its course and can last from a few days to a few years, at most. But you will get better."

I didn't completely believe him, but I clung to that promise with renewed hope. I drew it to my heart, hugged it close, repeated it, shared it with my family and said over and over again, "Thank you Father, I'm going to get better."

In time the "black hole" began taking on the appearance of a "valley." "Valleys" are not like holes. they're open-ended. They are temporary. And temporary means *it will end*.

Even what we sometimes call "terminal illnesses" are only temporary. There is nothing final for this rare breed of sheep called Christians.

The believer's life has no closures.

It's always open-ended.

the most "terminal" of human experiences is merely a door. Through that door, life begins again—only it's different. It's indestructible and forever.

All trips THROUGH the "valley" are temporary. They will end. And they will always end on a higher level than where they began.

> All discipline for the moment seems not to be joyful, but sorrowful; yet to those who have been trained by it, afterwards it yields the peaceful fruit of righteousness (Hebrews 12:11).

"Even Though I Walk Through The Valley Of The Shadow Of Death . . ."

*I*n the "valley," the fear is always greater than the reality.

Sheep are often spooked by harmless sounds and sights. A falling pebble, a fluttering bird, a puff of wind, a shout, even the bark of a dog can cause a sheep to run.

Did you notice the name of the "valley"?

It is not the VALLEY OF DEATH, it's THE VALLEY OF THE SHADOW OF DEATH.

It is often difficult to read this Psalm to someone who is ill. Mention of the word *death* sometimes suggests that I know something about the seriousness of their illness that they do not.

Many times when I read the word *death*, I can feel the fear as it creeps into the room.

This "valley" is not the valley of DEATH, it is only the valley of the SHADOW of death.

A SHADOW IS AN IMAGE WITHOUT SUBSTANCE.

Frightening? Yes!

Harmful? No!

Death is a shadow. It can appear harmful. But it's an image without substance through which we all walk. The "valley," however, is on THROUGH that which we all will walk.

Shadows are for walking THROUGH.

Its image may tower above us and around us, but as we approach it we will find that, like a shadow, it is powerless to stop us or harm us.

Often, I will talk to people who are dying. It's always easier when they know the truth.

After one has accepted the reality of death, it's then that the truth about death can be discussed.

I like to tell the dying that they are not going to die.

They usually answer by saying, "Yes, pastor, I am going to die. My doctor has told me I'm going to die."

"But you're not going to die."

"Yes I am."

But John 11 says YOU are not going to die.

Your body is going to die, but YOU are not.

I then quote these verses to them—

> Jesus said to her, "I am the resurrection and the life; he who believes in Me shall live even if he dies, and everyone who lives and believes in Me shall never die" (John 11:25, 26).

It says that the body is going to quit functioning for a while, but not the *person*. The body is temporary. The person is forever.

Death is only a shadow—an awesomely frightening shadow to be sure—but still only a shadow.

Death is the last enemy.

Sin's final judgment.

Satan's favorite weapon.

But it's only a shadow, and as we walk THROUGH, it becomes God's instrument to bring us to life.

If death is designed to bring us to life, can it really be all that bad?

The fear of death is great.

The fear, however, is far greater than the reality.

"I FEAR NO EVIL; FOR THOU ART WITH ME"

*S*heep never go "through the valley" alone.

An elderly nanny goat, sure-footed and alert, is usually in the lead. With its long white whiskers and spindly legs, a goat often proves to be the best animal to lead the sheep to the high places.

A goat can not only lead a flock over impossible terrain, but often, after lambing, it will offer its milk to orphaned lambs.

A castrated ram may also be used to lead.

An elderly ewe is always near the front to cause the young to follow.

A burro with a burro bell sometimes walks near the front.

Trained sheep dogs are scattered around and behind the flock to keep the wanderers from scattering.

If the flock is unusually large, the lead-shepherd may have others to assist him.

Sheep never move through places of danger alone.

The shepherd is always present.

Whenever we travel to a strange place, it's nice to have someone along who has been there before.

I recently spoke to a group of pastors and missionaries at the Camp of the Woods, high in the Adirondack mountains in upstate New York.

I had never been there before.

After landing in Auburn, I was met by friends who had planned to transport me.

"Where in the world is Camp of the Woods?" I asked.

"Just relax," they answered. "We'll show you. We go there every summer."

Whenever we travel to a strange place, it's nice to have someone along who has been there before.

I conducted a graveside service for a month-old baby whose parents were strangers to me.

As I walked across the windswept hill that wintry morning I wondered what I would say to that young, grieving couple huddled over the little white casket.

They didn't even lift their eyes when I introduced myself.

There was no response when I asked if I could be of any help.

After long clumsy moments of silence I said, "I'm sorry. I think I know how you feel. My wife and I lost our baby, too."

The young mother lifted her head, looked at me through her moist eyes and then threw her arms around my neck. She buried her head in my shoulder and sobbed as if her heart would break.

Why? She had found someone who had been there before.

Whenever we travel to a strange place, it's nice to have someone along who has been there before.

Not something. Someone.

A small boy complained about the darkness in his bedroom. He asked his mother to leave a light on. She replied, "Honey, you don't need to be afraid. God is with you."

The boy paused for a moment and then said, "Yes, Mother, I know God is with me. But, I'd sure like to have someone with skin on."

Not something. Someone.

We all need someone. Someone we can touch. Someone we can feel. Someone who will even be afraid with us. Someone with skin on.

There are times, however, when even someone with skin on is not enough. It's then we need SOMEONE.

SOMEONE has already promised.

"THOU ART WITH ME" is the timeless promise of the ever-present Shepherd.

It's the promise of the ONE who has been there before. Wherever your trip might be taking you, He has already been there.

*W*eapons, in the hands of friends, can be wonderfully reassuring.

Shepherds, in Bible times, are often pictured using staffs.

These staffs, or walking sticks, usually have large crooks at one end. The traditional staff is seen at Christmas time in the many pageants that depict the birth of Jesus.

This impractical type of staff is more fable than fact. A piece of hard wood with a natural crook or hook in it would be all but impossible to find. The traditional crook would also be too large to use in grabbing the hind leg of a sheep. The sheep hook has a crooked end, but usually the crook is smaller—just large enough to be wrapped around the sheep's leg and strong enough to hold it firm.

Usually the shepherd's staff was about four feet long, carved from an acacia or some other hard wood, and then used as a walking stick.

The shepherd became an artist at handling his staff. He could twirl it like a baton, use it to kill a rattlesnake or to clear the trail of cockleburs.

The stick was used in combat with feuding shepherds, or to kill predators intent upon harming the sheep.[1]

The rod was more like a club.

The shepherd used it constantly. It never left his hand.

Carved to fit his grip while young, the rod became an extension of the shepherd's arm and was used to protect and to inspect the sheep.

Weapons, in the hands of a friend, can be wonderfully reassuring.

Our Shepherd's rod is a symbol of His defensive power.

It may be the Word of His mouth that wilts an enemy.

It may be the strength of His right arm.

It may be a multitude of angelic beings.

It may be the force of nature.

It may be the protective armor He provides.

Whatever it may be, it's powerful and it's enough.

"God is able" are the words that describe the elaborate protective defenses of our Shepherd.

God, who set Himself between the fleeing Hebrews and the angry Egyptians, stands with whatever "rod" He chooses, and delivers us.

The staff is used to correct and to control the sheep.

Wandering sheep are often caught by the leg and redirected. A quick snap of the shepherd's arm can prevent an errant sheep from taking a fatal plunge over an embankment.

It can rescue one that has fallen in water, or lift one up that's beyond the shepherd's reach.

Disobedient sheep are prodded.

The prophet Isaiah describes us in terms we all understand, when he says,

> All of us like sheep have gone astray, Each
> of us has turned to his own way; (Isaiah
> 53:6)

There are mean, vengeful, gluttonous sheep, just like there are mean, vengeful, gluttonous people. They establish their own networks or "sheep societies." Their groups can range anywhere from two or three to twenty.

They form themselves into tight little groups and push and shove while the flock is grazing. They force themselves ahead of the others at the watering holes.

They are greedy and hostile and dangerous.[2]

There are "gay sheep."

An uncastrated ram will rape every sheep in sight, if not controlled.

There are the curious wanderers that often quietly slip off into the brush or lean out too far over the edge of an embankment in search of one more mouthful of grass, and then fall.

All these the staff corrects and controls.

Some liken the rod and the staff to the Word of God and the Spirit of God. This is most appropriate. Both the Word and the Spirit provide the Shepherd with powerful weapons with which to protect His sheep.

It's reassuring to know that whenever we go wandering, there is a unique tool, already designed, that will be used to bring us back where we belong.

Weapons, in the hands of a friend, can be wonderfully reassuring.

1. Irigaray, pp. 25, 26.
2. Ibid., pp. 28, 29.

"THOU DOST PREPARE A TABLE BEFORE ME IN THE PRESENCE OF MY ENEMIES"

*T*ables are for eating.

The "table" can refer to the mesas or the table lands, the plateaus or upper grazing areas that dot the highlands. After the summer snows have melted, they provide excellent forage.

Before one eats, the table must be set.

A shepherd will walk in advance of his flock or scout for days to find the most lush grass for feeding.

Water holes need to be located.

He will check for poisonous weeds and keep a sharp eye peeled for predators.

Sheep will not feed when fearful.

Sheep are unable to discern between the poisonous and the safe. The shepherd will remove the harmful and direct his flock toward that "table" which will provide maximum safety and serenity, as well as a diet that will fatten the sheep.

The eyes of sheep are strange and different from most other animals. They can't be fathomed. Sometimes they appear to be looking with curiosity, but usually, they appear disinterested—except when they are hungry. When hungry, they fix an accusing stare on the herder until he provides their food.[1]

Sheep need to eat.

Shepherds must go to great lengths to "prepare their table."

"Who sets the table at your house?"

"That all depends," you might answer.

"Depends on what?"

"It all depends on who's coming to dinner."

That's the way it was at our house, too. The children would often set the table. Even I could set the table unless someone very special had been invited. When someone special is scheduled, it's then that only someone special sets the table.

Place mats are replaced by linen. Crystal replaces glass. Cloth napkins replace paper ones. Only the best china and the best silver are used and they are placed in exactly the right position.

Candles are freshly fitted into their holders in preparation for lighting.

It all depends on who's coming to dinner, doesn't it?

Have you noticed who is setting the "table" in verse 5?

It's none other than our Shepherd.

The Lord is fixing dinner for me.

I must be someone pretty special to God.

Angels could be doing this job, but no, I'm so important that God does it Himself.

There are many comparisons between dumb sheep and their shepherds, but right here, those comparisons break down.

Dumb sheep don't eat with their shepherds.

But we do.

The analogy has been that of sheep and shepherds. Here it suddenly switches to a host and his guests.

What appeared at first to be just another meal, begins to look like a banquet.

One of the ultimate marks of friendship in Scripture is the experience of eating together.

Zacchaeus prepared a feast for the Lord after his forgiveness and then invited all his friends.

Lazarus prepared a feast for His Lord after his resurrection and then invited his friends.

Our Lord is preparing a feast for us. We are the honored guests.

When Jesus says, "Behold, I stand at the door and knock; if anyone hears My voice and opens the door, I will come in to him, and will dine with him, and He with Me" (Revelation 3:20), He is paying us the highest compliment.

He is granting us the greatest honor—that of having dinner with him.

A table is for eating, but His table is designed for even more. It is also designed to provide the most lasting and blessed fellowship available.

1. Irigaray, p. 29.

"Thou Dost Prepare A Table Before Me In The Presence Of My Enemies"

*S*heep are defenseless animals.

They can't bite like dogs, scratch like cats, kick like horses or even snap like turtles.

They are defenseless.

Yet their list of enemies is great.

Cougars will track sheep for days, returning to kill each day. Sometimes they will drag a dead sheep for miles to their lair.

A coyote will go to the weak side of a flock, grab a ewe or lamb by the throat and carry it away at speeds of up to forty miles per hour.

Pet dogs, even small poodles, can be more deadly than mountain lions.

Foxes will attack a newborn lamb and can stampede a flock.

Eagles will steal a small lamb.

Crows will pluck out sheep eyes.

Heavy fleece can protect a sheep from rattlesnakes, unless they are bitten on the snout while feeding.

Thorns can cause lameness.

Locoweed can cause blindness, paralysis, and death.

Aphids and butterflies can suck all the nurture out of the sheep's food.

Grapes can cause drunkenness.

A blowfly can lay eggs in an open wound that can lead to severe infection.

Sharp rocks can puncture sheep's paws.

Rain can cause them to stop eating, and approaching storms can create anxiety which causes them to overeat.

Locusts can strip the fields of forage in a matter of minutes.

A drought can make grazing fields impossible to find.

Rams can head-butt one another to death during breeding time.

Even the friendly trail dog can turn against the sheep and go on a killing spree that can be stopped only by the dog's death.

A small percentage of ewes in each flock will have a kidnapper instinct and will rob unsuspecting mothers of their newborn.

Sheep are defenseless against these enemies.

We have our enemies, too. Enemies that are intent upon our destruction. Some prey on us from without, some from within.

It is impossible to be free of them.

They surround us.

They hover over us.

They slither beneath us.

They live within us.

John, the apostle, identifies these enemies as,

1. The WORLD—the system that governs earth, built upon greed and controlled by myriad demonic beings that respond to the control of Satan. The world is always with us, reminding us that what we have is never quite enough.

2. THE FLESH—humanity's insatiable appetite inherited at birth and never completely controlled until stripped away at death.

3. THE DEVIL—the living being who opposes all that is God and all that is godly, who will go to any length to steal our affections from God and spirit our devotion away to himself.

The Lord's Table, set in the presence of these enemies, is designed to remind us that there is but One capable of protecting and preserving us.

Each time we hold that little wafer between our fingertips, and each time we place that small cup to our lips we acknowledge that our survival in a hostile world is only made possible by our Shepherd.

We are reminded that someday that table will be exchanged for another. The table of the future, set in heaven, will be far beyond the reach of the enemies that plague us now.

Until then, we'll pull up our chairs and we'll feast, and we'll trust that the power of the One whose name we celebrate will continue to be great enough to take care of the enemies that surround us.

Did you notice the change in pronouns as we moved through this Psalm?

The pronouns "He," "His," and "Him" are used five times in the first three chapters.

"He makes me lie down . . ."

"He leads me . . ."

"He restores my soul . . ."

"He guides me . . ."

". . . for His name's sake."

Those five pronouns suggest distance.

It seems that a proud sheep is pointing out his shepherd and describing those qualities that characterize him as faithful.

In verse four the "He" changes to "Thou."

The sheep who has been talking *about* his shepherd is now talking *to* him.

". . . Thou art with me"

"Thy rod and Thy staff, they comfort me . . ."

"Thou dost prepare . . ."

"Thou hast anointed . . ."

It seems that the sheep leaves its distant vantage point and ambles closer. Its nose nuzzles the shepherd's leg.

Its pride changes to adoration. It speaks directly and intimately to one it loves.

There is a meaningful lesson in worship here.

There are times for us to talk about Jesus.

There are times for us to talk to Jesus.

In talking to Him, or even better, *with* Him, we are

privileged to draw close and experience something that can never be enjoyed while "trailing."

John, in his first epistle, suggests a similar experience.

He describes a growing intimacy with Jesus that began with the ears,

> "What we have heard . . ."
> progressed to the eyes,
>> "what we have seen with our eyes ..."
> continued with a searching gaze,
>> "what we beheld . . ."
> and climaxed with a touch,
>> "What we have handled,
>> concerning the Word of Life . . ."

This progressive intimacy causes John to proudly invite his listeners and readers to join him, and behold the matchless glory and the breathless fellowship with Jesus that had become his proud possession (1 John 1:1-4).

He tells us that this is the only place of true joy.

I marvel every time I read the remarkable invitation in Hebrews 10:22. It's there that God invites us to ". . . draw near. . . ."

Our enviable sheep in Psalm 23 sounds like he has already heard and accepted just such an invitation. He assumes the attitude of adoration when he looks up into the shepherd's face, nuzzles his leg and says, "THOU art with me."

*S*hepherds watch a lot.

They watch the skies for changes in the weather, especially at shearing time. In early spring a sudden change in the weather can be disastrous to the shorn sheep.

Sheep can't stand rain or severe cold immediately after being shorn. It takes two or three days for the lanolin to thicken and protect the animal from a chill. Without that protection, dampness can penetrate to the tallow beneath the skin and cause death.[1]

They watch the sheep. If sheep suddenly begin to spread out and move away from each other, the watching shepherd can be reasonably sure that something, possibly a rattler, is in the center of the circle.

They watch for signs of restlessness, fear, and irritation.

They watch for signs of panic that could indicate the presence of the annoying nose flies.

Sheep, in summer, become frantic in their attempts to escape nose flies. They will run, they will toss their heads, they will try to hide in the brush, they will stamp their feet, they will refuse to graze.

Both the ewes and the lambs will stop eating, go off milking, lose weight and stop growing.

Phillip Keller says that, "Only the strictest attention to the behavior of the sheep can forestall the difficulties of "fly time." At the very first sign of flies among the flock he will apply an antidote to the heads."[2]

He used a remedy composed of linseed oil, sulfur, and tar. This was smeared over the sheep's nose and head to protect it from the flies.

The application of this remedy would cause an incredible transformation to take place. "Once the oil had been applied to the sheep's head there was an immediate change in behavior. Gone was the aggravation; gone the frenzy; gone the irritability and the restlessness. Instead, the sheep would start to feed quietly again, then soon lie down in peaceful contentment."[3]

In Israel, the mixture included olive oil.

Anointing in Scripture was not only limited to infested sheep.

People were anointed with oil. It was part of God's healing program.

It was also performed prior to any spiritual service.

Kings were anointed.

Priests were anointed.

Jesus was anointed.

At Jesus' anointing, the oil, which represented the Holy Spirit, gave way to a dove that descended from heaven and rested upon Him to announce the presence of the empowering Spirit in His life.

The anointing of the Holy Spirit in our lives is the means by which we are freed from the nagging irritations and frustrations of life.

Anointing doesn't mean the pouring of a solution over the head of a believer. It suggests a moment by moment appropriation of the Spirit's power to control the "pests" that bother us.

Only the Holy Spirit can quiet the irritations of life and create contentment.

Every Christian has the Holy Spirit. He can have no more of the Holy Spirit than was given him at the moment of conversion.

To possess the Holy Spirit and to be possessed *by* the Holy Spirit are two vastly different things, however.

To have the anointing oil of linseed and sulfur and tar at one's disposal meant nothing to the frantic sheep. The mere possession of the remedy never quieted the animals.

It's the application that counted.

To the believer this means an awareness of the Spirit's presence.

It also means the daily application, by faith, of the Spirit's power and control.

It means asking for the Spirit's fullness and control and then living under His direction.

It means bowing my infected head for a daily cleansing and submitting my rebellious will for a periodic purging.

It means being "filled" with the Holy Spirit moment by moment.

Only the Spirit of God can calm the irritations of life.

Only the Spirit of God can cause peace.

Only the Spirit of God can restore growth and vitality.

Summertime isn't the only time God's sheep need anointing.

We need it daily.

1. Irigaray, p. 194
2. Phillip Keller, *A Shepherd Looks at Psalm 23* (Grand Rapids: Zondervan, 1970), p. 116.
3. Ibid.

"My Cup Overflows"

*T*here is always more anointing oil than is needed.

As the shepherd pours oil over the head, rubs it onto the nose, and applies it to the wounds, something wonderful happens.

The animal's entire personality changes.

The irritability leaves.

Frustration ceases.

Hostility is gone.

The sheep begins to concentrate again on its purpose: to feed and to grow.

The nose flies of life are described in Galatians 5:19, 20 and 21. They are called the deeds of the flesh. There are fifteen of them.

IMMORALITY
IMPURITY
SENSUALITY
IDOLATRY
SORCERY
ENMITIES
STRIFE
JEALOUSY
OUTBURSTS OF ANGER
DISPUTES
DISSENSIONS
FACTIONS
ENVYING
DRUNKENNESS
CAROUSING

Seven are generally shunned by the Christian community. We take pride that we do not do them. Eight reflect the irritations of the flesh of which many of us are guilty.

These pests are constantly buzzing about us and within us, causing unceasing harassment. We can swat at them, run from them, and try to hide from them. We can pretend that they are not there—but we cannot eliminate them.

They create guilt and anxiety within and hostility without.

The only solution is found in Another.

My irritable personality must be exchanged for Another's.

What is commonly known as the fruit of the spirit is, in reality, the personality traits of the Holy Spirit. There are nine of them. They are listed in Galatians 5:22, 23.

LOVE
JOY
PEACE
PATIENCE
KINDNESS
GOODNESS
FAITHFULNESS
GENTLENESS
SELF-CONTROL.

The Holy Spirit pours His oil of LOVE over the nose fly of strife, and brings peace.

The Holy Spirit pours His oil of JOY over the nose fly of envy and brings peace.

The Holy Spirit pours His oil of PEACE over the nose fly of disputes and brings peace.

The Holy Spirit's anointing replaces my personality with His.

The results are dramatic—life-changing.

AND, THERE IS ALWAYS ENOUGH LEFT OVER FOR OTHERS.

THE OVERFLOWING CUP IS MEANT TO BE SHARED.

Why does my Shepherd cause my cup to run over?

In order that I might give some of this life-changing power to others.

The anointed head is for me.

The overflowing cup is for others.

"SURELY GOODNESS AND LOVINGKINDNESS WILL FOLLOW ME ALL THE DAYS OF MY LIFE"

*E*arly spring, in a sheep camp, is often the most satisfying time of the year. The grass is deep green and the lambs have gained in size until they weigh from fifty to sixty pounds. They play mindlessly. They leap and they frolic. Their energy, like a small child's, seems boundless.[1]

Autumn can be a special time. Now, free from nose flies and other bothersome pests, the sheep are fit and well and strong. Their time in the high country is about to come to an end. They have fed well and they have grown fat.

The springs and autumns in a sheep's life are the good times.

These are the times when they are most free from fear and danger.

These are the times when food is most plentiful.

These are the times when the weather is the most comfortable.

These are the times of "goodness."

These would be similar to the "good times" in the believer's life. Times when the children are small, and the fire is warm and the cupboard is full and the heart is at peace.

In these times we often say,

> The lines have fallen to me in pleasant places;
> Indeed, my heritage is beautiful to me (Psalm 16:6).

But there are the bad times.

A ewe can die and orphan a baby lamb.

A flood can drown the flock.

A storm can frighten the sheep and cause a stampede.

A drought can cause starvation.

Predators can destroy the animals.

These are the bad times.

For these times, the sheep need "lovingkindness" or "mercy" as it reads in some versions.

"Lovingkindness" is the word to describe the shepherd's provision in the time of need.

It, like mercy, is not just pity or sympathy or compassion, it is *intervention*.

The shepherd responds to the crisis and provides for the need.

When a ewe dies and a lamb is orphaned, the lamb is rejected by the rest of the flock. The only way another ewe will adopt it is by giving it the smell of her own. This requires stripping her own dead lamb of its skin and wrapping it about the orphan.

If this isn't possible, sometimes humans will adopt the lamb and bottle-feed it.

This is "lovingkindness."

This is the shepherd's provision for the bad days.

In the drought years, the shepherd will have to plan each day as if he were engaged in a war. Strategy requires plotting each movement of the flock to places where just enough forage is available for that day.

In the event of a dire emergency, stacks of cottonseed cakes are kept in the barn. The cakes are usually one inch rolls of cottonseed and corn meal with a binding of molasses.[2]

The sheep love them.

This is "lovingkindness."

This is the shepherd's provision for his sheep in time of need.

Cottonseed cakes remind me of what the Old Testament calls "manna"—the food which our Lord provided for the Hebrews during their lean times in the wilderness.

"Goodness" is God's provision during the good times.

"Lovingkindness" is God's provision during the bad times.

"Goodness" and "lovingkindness" are God's promised provision for all the seasons of life.

Regardless of what God has in store for us in the future, we can be assured of always having adequate provision for the present.

"Surely GOODNESS and LOVINGKINDNESS shall follow me all the days of my life."

1. Irigaray, p. 105.
2. Ibid., pp. 108-09.

". . . AND I WILL DWELL IN THE HOUSE OF THE LORD FOREVER"

*T*he word *and* is wonderfully important to this last verse of the Twenty-third Psalm. It connects the "goodness" and "lovingkindness" of our Lord in this life with His provision for us for eternity.

It connects our todays with our tomorrows.

It binds our present with our future.

It provides us with a lasting promise that our Shepherd is not only qualified to sustain us in all the "trailing" experiences of life, but He knows the way home and has a "sheepfold" awaiting us that is unlike anything we have ever known.

Three letters are all that are needed to build a bridge from now into our forever.

In this last phrase of David's Pastoral Psalm, we have finally come to the end of "trailing."

The long climb up "through the valley" is behind us.

The lambing and the shearing are over.

Winter is approaching.

It's time to go home.

I have a picture in my office of a ewe leaping for joy upon its return to the corral.

Its front legs are folded in against its body. Its hind legs are extended. Its head is outstretched. Its entire body is expectant.

It's home.

As we grow older, our hearts cry out for permanence.

We have lived through the changing seasons. We have survived changing relationships. We have endured changing our place of residence.

After so much change, we long for a home where death cannot invade and time cannot impair. A place where the important things of life remain and the unimportant disappear.

The entire Psalm is filled with change. Every phrase suggests movement. Every scene is a vivid word picture depicting our pilgrimage. Until this last verse—until our arrival home.

No visit anywhere on earth quite equals the joy of coming home.

Whenever we would travel with our children, each trip was a source of expectancy and delight. We would plan with enthusiasm, pack with vigor, and leave with excitement. After it was all over we'd hear that little phrase "we're home." Those words said it all—"of all the places we've ever been, home is the best."

In verse 6, we finally arrive "home." We reach the place of permanence. We've come to stay.

"The house of the Lord" in Psalm 23 is the same location Jesus speaks of in John 14 when He says, "I go to prepare a place for you." It's the same place John describes in the Revelation when he says,

> And he carried me away in the Spirit to a great and high mountain, and showed me the holy city, Jerusalem, coming down out of heaven from God, having the glory of God. . . . (Revelation 21:10, 11).

Heaven is a place on God's map. It's beyond the regions of all fancy. It's within the realm of the actual, the local.

It's not made of air.

It doesn't float around in some ethereal dream world.

It's not a Disneyland.

It's real, and—in contrast with earth—it's stable, secure, permanent and eternal.

It has been prepared for us as our very own residence for eternity.

There'll be no "want" there,
no forced rests,
no polluted water holes,
no preying predators,
no "valleys" of fear or danger,
no search for food,
no need for a rod or a staff, and
no cause for healing.

Heaven means different things to different people. We long for it for different reasons. It's a place, a real place, but it has different attractions.

To the poor it means wealth.
To the imprisoned it means freedom.
To the persecuted it means relief.
To the lonely it means friends.
To the dying it means life.
To all of us—imperfect ones—it's the promise
of perfection. We shall be like Jesus.

The frustration of failure, the agony of guilt, and the reality of sin will no longer exist. We will be free.

We will be home.

Our Shepherd will be there.

We will finally have the opportunity to thank Him for the good trip and for the safe arrival.

We will "dwell in the house of the Lord forever."

And then we'll all say it together,
"WE'RE HOME."

Bibliography

Bradbury, Margaret. *The Shepherd's Guidebook*. Emaus, Penn.: Rodale Press, 1977.

Irigaray, Louis and Taylor, Theodore. *A Shepherd Watches, A Shepherd Sings*. New York: Doubleday, 1977.

Jenkins, Marie. *Goats, Sheep and How They Live*. New York: Holiday House, 1978.

Keller, Phillip. *A Shepherd Looks at Psalm 23*. Grand Rapids: Zondervan, 1970.

Ponting, Kenneth. *Sheep of the World in Color*. England: Blandford Press, 1980.

Parker, Ron. *The Sheep Book: A Handbook for the Modern Shepherd*. New York: Scribner, 1983.

Thorpe, Denis. *The Shepherd's Year*. Vermont: David & Charles, 1979.

Towne, Charles Wayland. *Shepherd's Empire*. Norman, Okla.: University of Oklahoma Press, 1945.

About the Author

*D*on Baker is an Evangelical Free Church pastor in Rockford, Illinois, and also has served churches in Oregon and California. His numerous books include *A Fresh New Look at God; Acceptance; Beyond Forgiveness; Beyond Choice; Beyond Rejection; Depression; Pain's Hidden Purpose;* and *Heaven.*

About the Photographer

*T*he beautiful scenes from Israel in this volume were specially commissioned from international photographer Åke Lundberg. Lundberg has employed his photographic skills on every continent of the world and is perhaps best known for his work for *Decision* magazine and the Billy Graham Team. He now lives in Hillsboro, Oregon.